# What the Heck Do I Blog About?

## A Content Creation Coach Shares Her Secrets

Sue Allen Clayton

*Ciara!*

*Happy writing!*

*Sue Allen Clayton*

# Copyright

What the Heck Do I Blog About?
©2014 by Sue Allen Clayton

eBook published 2014 by Manorville Press, Manorville, New York
Printed book published 2015 by Manorville Press, Manorville, New York

ISBN: 978-0-9963476-0-0

Printed publication assistance provided by
Full Circle Press LLC (www.FullCirclePressLLC.com)

## Legal Notice

## Credits

Cover Design: Angie Zambrano

© February 2014 by Manorville Press, Manorville, New York

To reach the author, please email

**Sue@SueAllenClayton.com**

Sue Allen Clayton
Manorville Press
PO Box 1042
Manorville, NY 11909

# DEDICATION

To present and future bloggers: May you continue to building communities and sharing your passion!

Sue Allen Clayton

# Contents

# Introduction: Ready. Set. Nothing.

Does this seem familiar? You've carved out time to write a blog post, brewed yourself a cup of coffee, and are staring at an empty page or a blinking cursor. Despite your passion for a subject and great intentions to connect with your readers—you can't think of a single thing to say. Nothing. Not one word. Your mind is totally blank.

Whether you're blogging for business or personal reasons, it can be tough to come up with original content that connects with your readers. The good news is that your life is already full of potential blog posts. You just need to know where to look for ideas.

Fortunately, thinking of blog ideas is a skill you can learn. In fact, it's probably a skill you already have mastered in another area of your life. For instance, you may be a whiz at decorating and always scouring garage sales for unusual decorations. You could be a photographer who views every location as a place to photograph clients. Or perhaps you're a baker and always on the lookout for tasty ingredients for your cookies. In these cases, you've already trained your mind to be open to inspiration throughout your day.

You can apply the same skills to blogging. When you do, you'll see blogging ideas everywhere.

This book is set up in two parts. Part I will help you think like a blogger. You'll learn the secrets of successful blogging and how to develop a blogger's mindset.

In Part II, you'll find hundreds of blogging ideas that will inspire you to start writing.

Let's get started!

Sue Allen Clayton
**Sue@SueAllenClayton.com**

## Part I:
## How to Develop a Blogger's Mindset

Learning to think like a blogger does not require social media training or a journalism degree. You just need to develop a blogger's mindset.

So exactly what is a blogger's mindset?

A blogger's mindset is a belief that what you have to say is interesting and valuable to your readers.

Although that sounds obvious, there's a whole lot of I-wish-I-could-get-started bloggers who get stuck because they're afraid nobody will be interested in what they have to say.

While I can't guarantee that people will read your blog, I can say that you won't know unless you try. And the first step is to accept that you have something to say.

Fortunately, changing your mindset can be quick and pain-less. Have you ever had a two-year-old come to visit and realized that your house is not toddler-proof? Suddenly the pond in your backyard is no longer your outdoor oasis; it's the site of a potential drowning. Your mindset changes instantly!

In the next two chapters, you will learn how to change your mindset so that you think like a blogger. When you do, you'll find that you'll see the world in a different way and ideas will flow naturally.

## Build a Solid Foundation

When bloggers struggle to get ideas, it is usually because they are unsure of the purpose of their blog or are unwilling to share themselves with their readers. This chapter will explain how to get over both of these hurdles.

## State Your Purpose

What is the purpose of your blog? Take a moment and write down your answer.

If you couldn't answer immediately, take some time to think about it.

I know it's an overused metaphor, but it's tough to reach a destination if you don't know where you're going. It's the same with blogging. Knowing the purpose of your blog narrows down the scope of your posts and makes it easier to come up with ideas that are appropriate for your readers.

If you're blogging for fun, the purpose of your blog is probably obvious. You're writing to share your love of quilting, to record the homeschool journey of your kids, or to help stay motivated on your diet. (For the record, I've done all three.)

Personal blogs are easy to write when you're passionate and knowledgeable about your subject. You ask yourself, "What happened today?" and ideas flow naturally. Your readers get to enjoy your quilt projects, follow your homeschool journey, and maybe get a bit more motivated in their battle of the bulge.

If you're a business, the ultimate goal of your blog is to increase your profits. It's that simple. Every post should increase your visibility and ultimately entice people to buy your products, use your services, or come to your events.

Blogging is a way to communicate with your readers and to build a community. Both "community" and "communicate" are based on the Latin word "communis," which means "to share." Sharing is the foundation of blogging.

Learning to share can be tough for blog writers. Many of us were taught to keep our opinions to ourselves. We came to believe that what we had to say wasn't very interesting. And we learned to fade into the background.

Challenging these beliefs is can be tough, but you need to do it! It's pretty much impossible to build your visibility while you're trying to fade into the background.

At this point, let me be clear that you can decide exactly how much you want to reveal. You certainly shouldn't share anything you're not comfortable with.

It helps to recognize that your blog will attract a group of people with similar interests. So, although hearing about your stamp collection may bore the heck out of your spouse, your posts will be eagerly awaited by fellow phi-latelies. And, as you interact with your fellow stamp collectors, you will slowly grow comfortable. Even very private people are usually okay with talking about their pets, hobbies, and favorite foods!

Even if you're writing for business, your readers will still want to get to know you. They want to learn about your family, your hobbies and your passions. In fact, your story is what keeps your business blog from being a blatant advertisement for your products or services. It shows that you are unique and helps people understand why they should buy from you and not someone else.

Recently I was looking for a colo-rectal surgeon. (I know—yuck!) As I researched specialists, one of the doctors stood out. His blog revealed that, while he was in medical school, his father died of colon cancer. He switched his specialty to studying the lower part of the bowel and dedicated himself to eradicating this (largely) preventable disease. Guess who I chose as my new doctor?

This experience illustrates how blogging helped this doctor stand out from his colleagues. He had the same credentials as everyone else. However, because he shared his story and revealed a personal passion for his subject, he gained at least one new patient.

## THE SECRETS OF SUCCESSFUL BLOGGING

When my son was young, he had two totally different experiences with coaching. The swim coach was downright nasty; when she wasn't yelling, she was belittling the young swimmers. On the other hand, the bowling coach was always friendly and positive. She encouraged everyone on the team to do their best and celebrated every success with an enthusiastic "high five." Not surprisingly, my son grew to be a decent bowler and never developed his potential as a swimmer.

All of us have, at some point, internalized a "you're not good enough" message from a parent, teacher or coach and become our own critic. If you're critical of your writing, you'll find it virtually impossible to come up with blog ideas. Creative ideas rarely occur when you're fearful of making a mistake.

This chapter will help you move from "mean coach" to "nice coach" and to create an environment where you can generate ideas.

## IMPERFECT IS OKAY

You are not building a bridge or performing surgery. You are putting words on a screen (or page). The world will not end if you don't choose the perfect adjective or misplace a comma. So take the pressure off yourself. Write as well as you can, but don't aim to be nominated for a National Book Award.

## Be Yourself

The world already has a Donald Trump and a Steven Spielberg, so it's okay if you're not a real estate mogul or famous film director. Just be yourself. You may be naturally funny, zany or a daredevil. You may be a trendsetter and a leader in your field. Or you may be shy and serious, with responsibilities and interests that are far from fun. It's all okay. Be authentic and willing to share yourself.

## Clear the Past

When my clients share their high school horror stories, it's not about showering after gym class or nasty classmates in the lunchroom. They talk about English teachers criticizing their work. Even if you respected nothing else about this teacher, you internalized their belief that you could not write. It's now decades later and you're still self-conscious about your writing. You need to get over this!

First of all, remember that you were just a kid. There are probably a lot of things you believed when you were fifteen that you've re-evaluated. Having your own house and car, for example, are a whole lot less cool when you have to hold down a job just to pay for them!

Secondly, you need to understand that good blogging has little to do with English class. You're sharing your experiences, not researching and writing an essay! There's no need to impress anyone with your vocabulary or write 3,000 words about something you don't care about . Blogs are written in an easy, conversational style. You get to choose the length (shorter is better) and select a subject matter that you care about. If you can write an email to a friend, you can blog.

## Small is Beautiful

Many people believe that their lives are "not enough" to warrant blogging. After all, why blog about one child when there are other bloggers with twins, triplets, or septuplets? Why blog about your one-person CPA business when there are firms with hundreds of accountants? Or how can you share how you've overcome trauma, when you don't have a PhD?

This is another idea that needs to change.

Most bloggers do not lead very exciting lives or have impressive credentials. We go to work, have conflicts with our neighbors, and prefer watching TV to housework. We blog about the day-to-day events in a life that includes carpooling and barbeques, not exotic travel and Red Carpet events.

## It's the Journey, Not the Destination

Let's say you're an overweight, middle-aged mom who decides to train for a marathon. You start a blog and attract a following of wanna-be marathoners. Your readers do not just want a post about your time on Marathon day. Your readers want to share your journey—your trip to the sporting goods store for running gear, your run during a downpour, and why you hired a trainer. They want to know about the days you get up at 5 a.m. to run, and the days you say "screw it" and turn off the alarm. When you finally run the marathon, they will cheer you on and be excited to see how you do.

## Have a Place to Capture Ideas

My experience is that you can't schedule inspiration. Ideas usually show up during boring tasks that leave our minds empty, such as driving, shoveling snow, or showering. These ideas come quickly and, if you ignore them, leave your mind just as fast. The secret is to be prepared. Carry a journal in your purse. Keep index cards in the bathroom and beside your bed. Make sure your phone is accessible when you're exercising and use the dictate feature to capture ideas.

## Write in a No-Judgment Zone

Stop judging yourself and start writing. Don't censor yourself. Don't worry about your grammar, sentence structure, or word choice. Turn off your computer's spell and grammar checks, so you're not sidetracked by errors. If you can't think of the right word or need some additional research, insert some dashes and move on. And don't interrupt your flow by going down the rabbit hole of Internet research.

## Allow for Revisions

Recognize that a good idea is only the first step in writing a blog post. To prepare the final post, you'll need time to think, plan, write and revise. So give yourself time to do a good job.

# Part II:
## Exactly What Do I Write About?

One of my favorite quilt blogs is written by the owner of a large online quilt store. She travels around the world buying fabric and attending quilt shows. Within a month, her blog will contain photos of a quilt show in Tokyo, a selection of amazing fabric, and links to her many media appearances.

And then there's me. When I started my quilting blog in 2010, I was a hobby quilter from Long Island, who spent most of my day homeschooling both of my teenagers. My quilts were mediocre and I hadn't yet appeared in the media. Not exactly a riveting life! Yet I found enough material to publish more than 400 posts and developed a loyal following.

So what could these blogs possibly have in common? Quite a lot. We both write unapologetically about our lives and share ourselves with our readers. And we don't pretend to be someone we're not (although I must admit that her life is pretty awesome).

By now, I hope you've developed a blogger's mindset and are ready to come up with your own ideas. As you read through the next chapters, write down your ideas as you think of them. Stay in the "no judgment zone" and enjoy the process.

You do not need to be on a once-in-a-lifetime vacation to describe where you are. In fact, readers can relate better to photos of your neighborhood than pictures of the pyramids. Write about your location. Explain why it's significant or how it makes you feel.

Blog about your visit to a:

- ❖ Home Improvement Center, where the spring flowers inspire a post on how to plant your first garden, how to select top quality manure, or why you dislike getting dirt under your nails.

- ❖ Coffee Shop, where the hot apple cider inspires a post about your fifth grade class trip to an apple orchard, how to make apple pie, or why apple butter is a healthy alternative to peanut butter.

- ❖ Warehouse Club in August, where you're annoyed that the school supplies have already been replaced by Christmas decorations. This inspires a post about your biggest pet peeves, why you love (or hate) holidays, or why you felt compelled to buy an electric blanket when the temperature is above ninety degrees.

- ❖ Thrift Shop, where you are excited to discover a great selection of antique linens. This inspires a post about how to use vintage fabrics as artwork. You can write about your family dinners at grandma's house, where your job was to press the tablecloth and napkins before your cousins arrived. Or you can write about the pain of donating your "thin clothes" to a local thrift shop.

- ❖ Local Events, such as festivals, tournaments, concerts, blood drives, or parades. You can share highlights of the event, explain why you chose to attend, or profile one of the participants.

- ❖ Dermatologist, which inspires a post on how your addiction to tanning damaged your skin.

- ❖ Nursing Home, where you learn that your mom's best friend is moving to another facility. This inspires a post about your best friend, the challenges facing the elderly, or how to adapt your home to accommodate a wheelchair.

- ❖ Fitness Center, which inspires posts about how to stay motivated to work out, the importance of exercise during pregnancy, or how you justify buying donuts on the way home from the gym.

- ❖ Grocery Store, where the artfully displayed eggplants lead to posts about using purple as a bedroom color scheme, how to convince your teenage daughter to eat vegetables, or why you refuse to buy genetically modified vegetables.

## 2. Take Your Readers Backstage

When my son was in first grade, he was dying to see inside the teacher's lounge at his school. He was convinced it was a luxurious retreat that even contained a hot tub! Although the plastic chairs and outdated décor were not very exciting, it shows that even children are fascinated with what's behind closed doors.

Behind-the-scenes tours are extremely popular. People willingly spend their vacations touring factories that make Crayola crayons, Hershey chocolate, or Ben and Jerry's ice cream. As a quilter, I have enjoyed several behind-the-scene tours that included fabric manufacturers and costume designers.

Thankfully, you do not need to be a multi-million dollar business to give readers a glimpse into the back office of your world. Even a home-based, solopreneur can come up with ideas and share:

- ❖ **Special Delivery.**
  Recently my daughter received an unexpected gift package containing *Harper's Bazaar Magazine* clippings from 1899 to 1907. Since both of us write fabric-related blogs, this was perfect to share with our readers. A lot of my quilter colleagues share photos of their fabric deliveries, which are eventually transformed into quilts. This morning, UPS delivered my TurboTax software so that I can complete my income taxes. Not exciting, but certainly something every taxpayer can relate to and worthy of a post.

- ❖ **Snippets of Your Day.**
  Snap a photo of your messy (or clean) desk, the snow on your car, or the "To Do" list on your whiteboard. Describe a conversation you overheard at the coffee shop. Share your opinion on an article that you found online.

- ❖ **Describe a Process.**
  You may not own a factory, but you have a method for doing business. Describe how you negotiate the price of a venue, set up a photo shoot, or choose the freshest flowers for your bouquets.

- ❖ **Share What You've Learned.**
  I've had hip problems for more than ten years, caused by a lack of both strength and flexibility in my legs. Over the summer, I was researching muscle strength and learned that the most common reason that people go into assisted living is lack of leg strength. Since this is of interest to my readers, who are generally women over fifty, I blogged about my own challenges, my new-found knowledge, and a couple of my favorite books about strength training.

- ❖ **Talk About Your Suppliers.**
  If you're a caterer who buys from local farms, post about where you get your ingredients. If you're a massage therapist who uses all natural products,

tell your readers why they should avoid chemicals on their skin. I frequently recommend online fabric suppliers, including one retailer that has high prices, slow delivery and mediocre customer service. (I recommend them because they've got a huge selection of fabrics and an excellent website.)

❖ **Special Days.**
Tell your readers about days that are significant for your business, such as your anniversary of founding your business. I know of a local nail salon that was named after the partners' mothers, both whom died of cancer. This story could inspire a great post for Mother's Day, one of their birthdays, or during Breast Cancer Awareness Month.

❖ **Pet Stories.**
Pet stories are well-received and generally uplifting. I have three miniature dachshunds who sleep in a portable baby crib in my office. Every once in a while, I'll share a photo of them sleeping with their feet up in the air, or stacked on top of each other like seals.

❖ **Changes To Your Office.**
You might be painting your workspace, getting new furniture, or changing your artwork. Last summer, I took a break from blogging to re-arrange our home and move my office to a different room. Even though it made my house look like an episode of "Hoarders," I shared photos of the stacks of fabric and books around my house.

## 3. WRITE A REVIEW

Reviews are quick to write and totally appreciated by readers. As an avid quilter, I have spent thousands of dollars after reading reviews of the fabrics, patterns and quilting gizmos. I know this is equally true for friends who are photographers, athletes, and fashionistas.

The good news is that you probably already own a large selection of products that you already have an opinion about.

Write a blog post to review:

- ❖ Books, magazines and blogs.

- ❖ Local events and attractions.

- ❖ Helpful YouTube videos.

- ❖ Conventions, trade shows, seminars and training programs.

- ❖ Software, hardware, gadgets and tools that make your job easier.

- ❖ Vendors and suppliers.

- ❖ Retailers that provide fast shipping, great prices, and/ or first-rate customer services.

- ❖ Organizations, charities or foundations.

- ❖ Hobby-related products and gear.

- ❖ Phone apps

- ❖ Hotels, restaurants, and bars.

- ❖ Movies, plays, and concerts.

## 4. Check Your Calendar

There are special days every month that can inspire posts. You'll find both traditional and unusual holidays at www.holidayscalendar.com. Here are some examples of how holidays can inspire your posts:

- ❖ **New Year's Day.**
  This celebration is held on January 1. Share your resolutions and goals for the coming year. Recap suc-

cesses and failures from the last year. Describe how you set goals and how you plan to stay on track over the next 12 months.

❖ **Valentine's Day.**
February 14 is traditionally the day we celebrate love. Profile a couple who've been married for more than fifty years. Showcase your products that contain the color red. Write about how exercise has helped strengthen your heart.

❖ **Tax Freedom Day.**
This is the day, which occurs the last half of April, that the average American has earned enough income to pay their tax obligations for the year. Tax Freedom Day is the perfect day to blog about ways to reduce taxes or to how to use couponing to stretch your salary.

❖ **Earth Day.**
Celebrated on April 22, Earth Day is a world-wide event to promote environmental protection. The first Earth Day was held in 1970. Blog about where you were in 1970. Share how you will celebrate Earth Day (or why you choose not to). Describe the value of community gardens and how they help the environment.

❖ **Memorial Day.**
Held on the last Monday of May, Memorial Day honors men and women who died in the United States Armed Forces. Tell the story of a family member's military service. Describe your best-selling merchandise that is red, white and blue. Share your family's Memorial Day barbeque tradition, including your mother's recipe for potato salad.

❖ **Book Lover's Day.**
Held on August 9, Book Lover's Day celebrates reading and encourages people to relax with a good book. Share your earliest memory of reading, recommend

one of your favorite books, or share a book that changed your life.

❖ **National Peanut Day.**
Held on September 13, this holiday is held in South Africa to honor the peanut industry. Share a family recipe for peanut brittle. Describe life with a nut allergy and why airlines shouldn't serve peanuts as snacks. Explain why crunchy peanut butter is vastly superior to smooth.

❖ **Halloween.**
Halloween is celebrated on October 31 and began as a way to remember the dead. Blog about the scariest movie you've ever seen. Describe your first Halloween costume. Write about your favorite Halloween candy — and whether you have any tricks to keep yourself from bingeing on chocolate.

❖ **Boxing Day.**
Boxing Day occurs on December 26 and is celebrated in Commonwealth countries, including Canada, Hong Kong and Australia. Since I'm originally from Canada, I knew that Boxing Day originated when servants received "gift boxes" from their employers. Blog about a holiday from your heritage or a special occasion celebrated by your family.

## 5. Comment on Current Events

If you're struggling for blog ideas, glance through your local newspaper or visit a national news website. You'll find a wealth of ideas, such as:

❖ **Births and Deaths.**
For weeks in 2013, the world waited for Princess Kate to give birth to the next generation of British royalty. This could inspire posts about how to select the best wall color for your nursery, a description of

your battles with infertility, or a discussion of how to use men's clothing for maternity wear.

❖ **Celebrities.**
As I write this, 19-year-old Justin Bieber has just been arrested for the second time in one week. (He was charged with drunk driving in Miami and assaulting a limousine driver in Toronto.) This can inspire posts on why we need stricter enforcement of drunk driving laws, a time when you were disappointed by a celebrity idol, or a choice you made that you now regret.

❖ **Disasters.**
Unfortunately there are a lot of disasters – including tsunamis, oil spills and shootings – to write about. When Hurricane Sandy devastated my region of Long Island in 2012, I wrote many posts about how our area was coping. It had little relation to my usual blog subject of quilting, but it was in the news and my readers appreciated my perspective. Your blog post may be about how to protect your home from a hurricane or how local wildlife was affected by a forest fire.

❖ **Fairs and Festivals.**
Every region has some cool local events. Our region has an annual Fleece and Fiber Fair that features animals, such as alpacas and chinchillas, that are used for wool. There's also a Horseradish Festival with a recipe contest, cooking demonstrations, and competitions. Even a visit to a pet adoption event can inspire posts about how to select a non-allergenic dog breed, your adventures in adopting a stray cat, or how you dealt with the death of a child's hamster.

❖ **Politics.**
Long Island is overpopulated with white-tail deer. These animals cause car accidents (including one with my husband's vehicle), damage commercial

crops, and destroy home gardens. As a result (according to a *Newsday* article by David Schwartz published on December 9, 2013), local towns have contracted with USDA sharpshooters to kill from 2,000 to 3,000 deer from a herd of 30,000. This local story could inspire a variety of posts. Share why you agree (or disagree) with the cull. Write about a time when wildlife caused damage to your property. Share why you feel that hunting is necessary or why you believe that animal rights need to be protected

❖ **Sports.**
Whether it's your child's volleyball team or the Olympics, sports can triggers lots of ideas for posts. Describe the time your son broke his arm ice skating. Write about the importance of your Thursday night bowling league. Tackle childhood obesity and describe how you'd increase activity in kids who prefer video games to riding bikes.

❖ **Scandals.**
Although I currently live in New York, where we have plenty of our own scandals, I spent my first thirty years of life in Toronto, Canada. As a result, I've followed the antics of Toronto's crack-smoking mayor, Rob Ford, with interest. Watching him can inspire posts about an embarrassing relative, an experience that served as a wake-up call in your life, or a time that you were unjustly accused.

❖ **Weather.**
I'm writing this book during an unusually cold winter with lots of snow. While it's old news to my neighbors in New York, my friends in warmer regions love to hear about the trials of winter. Share the rain, snow or sunny skies in your area and write about how you're coping with the weather.

It doesn't matter what kind of business you run—whether you're a yoga instructor, a graphic designer or a landscaper—your customers will likely love being featured on your blog. (Of course, you'll need to ask permission first!) Here are some ideas for blog posts:

❖ **Profile Your Customers.**
If you're a landscape architect, showcase some of your customer's gardens and explain why they chose specific plants. If you're a dress designer, profile a client in one of your custom wedding gowns and describe why she insisted on a lace bodice. If you teach art, select a student, highlight their work, and explain why they like to work with pastels.

❖ **Share Achievements.**
Did one of your clients win an award, participate in a charitable event, or write a book? Write a blog post about this customer and explain the story behind their success.

❖ **Describe the Solution.**
Describe a customer's problems and how you solved it. Share the story of before they met you, what happened as you worked together, and the final outcome. Explain how you helped a customer reduce their utility bills, find the perfect bra, or hire a nanny. Share how you helped a business reduce staff turnover, plan an event, or redesign their website.

❖ **Before and After's.**
Unlike describing a solution, before and after posts just highlight the beginning and end points of a journey. If you're a professional organizer, take photos of an office before and after it was organized. If you're a fitness trainer, share a client's photo before and after they lost thirty pounds. Or if you're an aesthetician, show how a client's acne improved before and after

treatments. Readers love transformations because they are educational and inspirational.

## 7. Share Your Knowledge

How many times have you searched online for information that you can use? Since my hobby is quilting, I constantly refer to blog posts that describe how to make mitered corners or the dimensions of hanging sleeves. Yes, this information serves a very specific niche -- which is exactly what you are looking for! You can share:

❖ **"How To" Instructions.**
 Tell people how to tighten a toilet seat, design their own wedding bouquet, or make low calorie yogurt.

❖ **Your Experiences.**
 Perhaps you've just baby proofed your home, recovered from a serious illness, or declared bankruptcy. Describe what you did well, and what you'd do differently.

❖ **Checklists.**
 Write a checklist on how to select the perfect eyeshadow, the supplies needed to manicure your own nails, or how to avoid the major causes of tooth decay.

❖ **Resources.**
 Because I homeschooled for nine years, parents often ask me for advice on how to get started. I send them a resource list that includes my favorite "how to" homeschooling books, links to online support groups, and recommendations for curricula. These resource lists are always appreciated, especially by people who are brand new to a subject.

❖ **Reviews.**
 Everything can be reviewed, including books, videos, products, phone apps, retailers, hotels, hair dye, vitamins, and dog breeds. (See pages 19–20 for more.)

❖ **Takeaways.**
  Describe what you learned from an event, clinic, or training class. Every day I receive emails offering training, coaching, seminars, eClasses, books and more. While most of these sound wonderful, I have limited time and resources. So I really appreciate the input of people who've blogged about their experiences.

## 8. Highlight Your Mistakes

I was surprised to discover, when writing my quilting blog, that the most popular posts were about things I'd done wrong. I have shared quilts where I've selected the wrong thread color, made serious cutting errors, and generally messed up the design. The bottom line is that readers want to know that you are human! So have a sense of humor and allow readers to learn from you. You can share:

❖ A mistake that caused you to be fired from your first job.

❖ How designing your own website ultimately cost you more money.

❖ A fashion faux-pas.

❖ How you arrived unprepared for your first trade show.

❖ The way to handle a bad haircut.

❖ How overtraining at the gym lead to an injury.

❖ Why you should (or should not) use a contractor who is not licensed.

❖ The worst advice you ever received.

❖ How a fad diet ruined your health.

❖ Why clipping coupons does not save you money.

❖ How hiring the wrong employee almost ruined your business.

## 9. GET PERSONAL

When you blog regularly, readers grow to care about your family and your community. Last year, my readers were extremely supportive when I underwent major surgery and changed the direction of my business. Here are some suggestions of big events to blog about:

❖ Birth of a child or grandchild.

❖ Engagement, wedding or anniversary celebrations.

❖ Sending your child to kindergarten, high school or college.

❖ Buying a new home, finding an apartment, or downsizing.

❖ Important anniversaries or milestones.

❖ Changing locations, jobs or businesses.

❖ Surviving surgery and health challenges.

❖ The death of someone close (including pets).

❖ Graduations, accomplishments and awards.

You can also blog about very minor events, such as:

❖ Preparing for your first garage sale.

❖ Having coffee with your daughter-in-law.

❖ Learning how to download apps to your new cell phone.

❖ Putting your cat on a diet.

❖ Buying a bookcase.

- ❖ Psyching yourself up for dental work.

- ❖ Seeing a great (or terrible) movie.

- ❖ Wrapping a gift.

- ❖ Buying a lottery ticket.

- ❖ Searching for car keys.

## 10. Photos Are Fabulous

There's no rule that says your blog needs to be a certain number of words. In fact, I have seen many successful blogs that contain only photos and a catchy headline. This can be a very successful strategy, so keep your camera ready!

Here are examples of a descriptive headline to accompany photos:

- ❖ Teaching in Toronto

- ❖ Packing for Summer Camp

- ❖ Spring Fabrics Have Arrived!

- ❖ Trick or Treating

- ❖ First Snowfall

- ❖ Dinner is Served

- ❖ 5K Fun Run

- ❖ Moving Day

- ❖ Here's What I've Been Up To

- ❖ Coffee Break

## Conclusion

I hope this book helped you develop a blogger's mindset and recognize that inspiration is all around you.

Please visit my website at SueAllenClayton.com for more information.

Happy Blogging!